Turning Left:
An Immigrant's View of the Puzzle

By: Pedro (Pete) Diaz

I dedicate this book
To my amazing parents
Who sacrificed everything
To insure my future

Turning Left:
An Immigrant's View of the Puzzle
First edition 2016

Editor:
Annie Willis, MEd,Doctoral Candidate

Interior design and composition
Pedro (Pete) Diaz

Cover design
Pete Diaz & Ivonne Diaz

ISBN: 978-1533525222
ISBN: 1533525226

Turning Left:
An Immigrant's View of the Puzzle

I was ten years old when soldiers came to our family's apartment in Havana to inform us that Castro had approved our departure from Cuba to the United States of America.

Eight years earlier, my parents had applied to the U.S. for political asylum. Although the American government had approved our permanent visa, Castro had yet to decide if he would let us leave Cuba.

When a Cuban citizen decides to leave Cuba, the Cuban government regards that person as a traitor to their country. The waiting period to grant an exit from Cuba can become an unsettling time for the citizen.

I will never forget what it feels like to lack the most essential human right, the right to be free.

Not free as in doing what the heart desires. This freedom is an essential freedom and is expressed in what I consider to be the holiest of all documents, the United States Bill of Rights.

After waiting eight long years, the Cuban government decided that we could leave our country.

Many Americans have forgotten that only ninety miles from our shores lies a country that, once graced with first-class status, has been stripped of all dignity by a tyrant regime; a dictatorship that enslaves its own people.

Living today in America's modern society has caused me to believe that very few millenials are interested in the direction our government is heading.
The leftist wave in our nation today, with its political correctness, can be a danger to our moral fibers.

A person who has lived through the consequences of socialism can see what is to be an inevitable conclusion to our trip down the road of social progression.

Cuba was not always a communist country. Having been colonized by Spain for four hundred years, Cuba finally rose up in arms and acquired its freedom and independence in 1898. Much like America's liberation from England, the people fought for freedom.

Between 1898 and 1959 Cuba enjoyed the spoils of a prosperous nation. Hard-working Cuban citizens and a strong American ally gave way to earning the island its name, "The Key of the Antilles".

Cuba's geographical location once gave merchants a great trade advantage between the American continents. The island's tropical climate enabled a successful crop and tourist industry.

As with many societies, success did not come without corruption. The gap between the wealthy and the poor propagated and the people yearned for change.

While change may sometimes seem like the answer, it can often create a new set of problems.

Castro's promise of change and social equality sparked a firestorm among the youth of Cuba, leading to the revolution that overthrew President Batista's government. While President Batista's government had its share of problems, it was nothing compared to what was to come.

Change did not happen overnight. The press and progressive university professors advocated social reform in the classrooms and turned the youth into a furious movement that chipped away at the capitalist political system.
Protest after protest, citizens of a lower socioeconomic status continued to demand unearned resources.
Rich industrialists were deemed as Goliath, while the poor and uneducated were seen as David.

After a period of political correctness and violent opposition, it was easy for Fidel Castro to sweep into power using elaborate and mesmerizing speeches, many lasting for hours at a time. Social equality had become a reality with its core being shared wealth.

Businesses, especially foreign, were confiscated by the new government of Castro and their owners were driven away. Professionals, including doctors and lawyers, became employees of the state and were given a salary comparable to the low farmers' pay. High-prized estates were confiscated and distributed among the poor.
As this form of socialist economy fell into debt, the government nationalized the banking industry and took Cuban citizen's money for the revolution's cause.

Socialism in a society means equal nothing for "all". In his "Europe Unite" speech, Winston Churchill states, *"Socialism is the philosophy of failure, the creed of ignorance and the gospel of envy. Its inherent virtue is the equal sharing of misery"*.
For the poor, this was not a problem at the moment. For the nation, it was a disaster.

The country's infrastructure collapsed and the so-called free education and healthcare system became third-rate. A country once credited for the advancement against yellow fever could no longer afford to treat the common cold.

As the eyes of Cubans began to open to the reality of a failed political system, Castro took matters to a new level. The military went through a modification transition wherein many of the brass were executed and replaced with Castro's revolutionary guards.
Guns were confiscated from citizens for the purpose of national security. To avoid a massive exodus, traveling outside the country became prohibited.
To help him enforce control, Castro desperately turned to Russia for support and the Marxist / Leninist agenda invaded Cuba.

During the Cuban Missile Crisis, in October of 1962, an agreement was made between the U.S. and Russia. In order to come to a peaceful resolution and have Russia withdraw their nuclear arsenal from Cuba, President John F. Kennedy agreed to prohibit the United States of America from invading Cuba. This pact would seal the fate of the Cuban people forever.
This decision resulted in the loss of the lives of many Cuban and American fighters, trained by the CIA, to overthrow Castro in the Bay of Pigs invasion. The soldiers attacked the beach at the Bay of Pigs in Cuba and according to the CIA plan, were intended to receive American air

support, although due to the new agreement, it never came. Shortly after this episode, the U.S. agreed to grant political asylum to any Cuban defector.

All American companies in Cuba were taken over by Castro's government. Because of the Kennedy/Khrushchev agreement, Americans were not able to recuperate their assets.

Inevitably, as it has happened in other countries, socialism became communism. The economy failed. Unemployment skyrocketed. The Peso, once at the same value of the dollar, lost its value completely. In order to feed the masses and maintain control, the federal government became the dictating force in Cuban lives.
The courts became occupied by government officials. The lame duck congress and senate was turned into a court-martial tribunal in which any opposition to Castro was dealt with harshly and eliminated.

 In order to maintain his grip on Cuba's citizens, Castro assumed that he should begin the training of his citizens at an early age.
Education became indoctrination. Textbooks were replaced with communist propaganda. The press was censored. Neighborhoods were monitored by individuals called "agents of the revolutionary defense committee". Much like the neighborhood

"gossip", these agents would report any suspicious activity to the police.

Conservatism became the enemy. Castro used race as a divider among citizens.
Castro's revolution encouraged citizens to change the racial makeup of the island in the name of diversity. Castro distributed racial propaganda through a massive media campaign. The new motto declared that in order to be equal, whites and blacks must engage in interracial relationships. Citizens who expressed their disagreement with this notion were labeled "racists." It all seemed unrealistic.

The dream

I was ten years old when our freedom arrived at our Havana apartment, but my story does not begin there.
My story begins with one man's dream of a better life for his family.

The idea of the "American Dream" is a concept pursued by many, including my father.

My father left Cuba for New York City at the age of nineteen in search of fortune. He procured a job and an apartment and once established, he sent for my mother.

My parents' plan was to make enough money to return to Cuba and open up a public cafeteria. When my mother became pregnant with me, my parents decided to go to Cuba to have a Cuban child. After all, that was their heritage.

In 1958, shortly after my birth, my family returned to the U.S. to continue with their plans.
Things were not perfect and it was hard to adjust.

The fast-paced American way of life was stressful, especially because of my parents' language barrier. However, hard work and struggle in America had rewards and my parents believed that the benefits outweighed the cost.

In 1960, Castro's promise of a better life and my grandfather's death led my parents to decide to return to Cuba and pursue their dream of owning a public cafeteria. This decision would be one they regretted their entire lives.

Shortly after our arrival, strange things began happening in Cuba. Castro's military began expanding into the towns. Businesses were obligated to "cooperate" with the revolution, both monetarily and voluntarily.
The government started forming neighborhood watchdogs. These watchdogs were given a salary from the Castro government. They wore military uniforms even though they were civilians.
Community organizers would come to our house and "persuade" my family to come to public events and rallies.
Each time Castro spoke publicly, the community organizers would charter buses for transportation to the event. These buses would go to the work centers and pick up workers to take them to Castro's event. If citizens refused to go, their pay for that day would be withheld from their salary. If the establishment's owner refused to let the workers go, the community organizers would organize a violent protest against the company. These rallies would last up to hours at a time. Castro, an eloquent speaker, would mesmerize the people of Cuba.

Castro recruited some of the most poor citizens for these organizing roles. Professionals in many public agencies were replaced by uneducated people. These people had been desperate for power and now they had authority.

Growing up, my dad attended a Catholic school. He matriculated through a church charity that would grant scholarships to the local poor.
My dad tells of the generosity of the school director who granted a scholarship to a very poor young man from his town. My father watched how the director took this boy under his wing, turning his life around from hopelessness to a bright future.
Upon the revolution, the director was ironically replaced by the young man he had sponsored. The director, now unemployed, went to see his protégé for a job. The ungrateful pupil discarded his mentor. He told the former teacher that under the new revolution there would be no preferential treatment for anyone.
This can be what happens when people are given unearned rewards and power.

Upon the realization of Castro's lies, my parents applied for political asylum to the United States. It was then the devil came upon my family.

Immediately upon my parent's application to leave the country, my father lost his job.

He was sent to do forced labor at an organization called MICON, which stands for ministry of public works. There, my father's soft hands were destroyed by the pick and the shovel.

My father was gone for days at a time. From our neighborhood, he would take a public bus to an adjacent town. There, a train would take him to the section of the country that needed roadwork or to a field to harvest sugarcane.

My father would return for a few days at a time and would tell my mother stories about his work on the roads or in the field. I would listen from my room, pretending to be asleep.

My father told of the blistering sun scorching his arms and neck as he swung a machete, diagonally from top to bottom, cutting down the sugarcane just a few inches above the ground. After hours of cutting, another group of workers would come and collect the stalks for transport to the refinery. Swinging the machete was exhausting. The cane stalks were up to 13 feet tall and my dad felt lost inside an endless jungle with no visibility.
The only sight, inches from his face, was a multitude of thin, yellow poles of sugarcane. Dad used to say that a man could become a diabetic just by walking through the thick sugar maze.
Without the advancement of modern machinery, harvesting sugarcane was brutal work. The work

at some of the sugarcane fields became so difficult that some workers, in order to be medically discharged, would wield their machetes into their own legs.

I have few memories of my infancy and it could be possible that my mind protects me from the horrible trauma a full recollection would cause me. However, I do remember enough to formulate my convictions. The memories of my childhood struggles due to my parents' anti-revolutionary ideals have been burned into my senses forming me as a person. These experiences have contributed to awakening my fears upon witnessing the apathy of the millennial generation in America.

Childhood was difficult in Cuba. The things we take for granted in the U.S. were an essential part of survival during my childhood.
Being an outspoken person is something that was unimaginable to me back then. The idea that a person has the right to complain about the treatment of a police officer would have been outrageous to me as a child.
When I learned that a U.S. citizen can own and use a gun to protect themselves without fear of reprisal, it was as absurd to me as an Alfred Hitchcock story.

The Injustice

During my time in Cuba, a person who decided to leave the country was considered a traitor. Citizens were continuously monitored. Our thoughts were censored. Citizens were continuously threatened by government officials with the possibility of denying their exit from Cuba. Under this threat, the Cuban citizen was subjected to a constant mental abuse. Although our family was also subjected to this threat, my mother would trade handmade clothes for food in the black market knowing that if she were to be caught, our family would lose our chance of freedom.

I remember traveling on a bus when a communist soldier in a green uniform demanded that my mother get up from her seat so that he could sit, acting as if my mother was a second-class citizen. At first, my mother just looked away from the man without moving. A woman of great conviction, my mom never stepped away from a fight. Having been a one of eight children and raised by a merchant marine, she was a force to be reckoned with.

Witnessing my mom's defiance, the man in green looked around the bus to see the passenger's reactions. The passengers had all become quiet and tuned into the scene.

The cowardly soldier once again demanded that my mom get up, this time with his right hand resting on his holster, where he kept a military issued Colt .45 pistol.

The bus driver, who had been peeping through the rear-view mirror, stopped the bus on the side of the road, applied the parking brake and turned around on his chair to witness the spectacle. My mother slowly and calmly gathered her bag, took me by the hand and stood up to proceed to the rear of the bus. The soldier took my mother's seat and looked out his window. His leg was shaking and his lips were trembling with anger, or fear. I still do not know for sure.

The anger of a young boy at this indignity was only defused by the pressure of my mother's hand holding tightly around my arm. I did not realize it then, but today I understand that she was protecting me from the consequences that my protest would have caused, the loss of our opportunity to leave Cuba. Only a strong woman would let herself be humiliated in order to protect my future.

Cuba had become an intolerant nation, slowly stripping away the rights of citizens.

In America, our children can stand up for any cause, even for the rights of animals, without fear of reprisal. It is important to protect these rights.

Mission Impossible

After the sugarcane was harvested, my father would take a break to come home. He took this opportunity at home to do some odd jobs around the community in order to sustain us. Dad would repair a door for someone or re-screen a window, although he had never been a handyman. He learned by trial and error in order to provide extra financial support for my family.
When work was scarce, dad would take us on the road exchanging mom's handmade clothes for food. We would travel from place to place as a family, wanting to make up for his long absences.

In Cuba, people mostly travel by bus. Not many people can afford to buy a car, much less pay to maintain it. While these trips were a form of distraction for me, they were covert missions for my parents.

Frequently, I would notice the nervousness of my parents. Sometimes the route and circumstances of our trips would confuse me. We would get off of one bus only to get on another going in the same direction. We would stop at a stranger's house and only stay long enough to drink some Cuban coffee, a strong type of espresso that Cubans drink in small one ounce cups frequently throughout the day. After the brief stop, we would get on the next bus to head home.

While I enjoyed the view from the bus window, my parents carefully scouted the bus for anyone who looked suspicious. Anyone on that bus could be a government agent or simply a tattletale who could ruin our lives if we were discovered carrying the bag, or "Secret Package".

Our family carried a bag on all of these trips. The bag we brought home was always different than the one we left the house with. Sometimes, I noticed a funny smell coming from the mysterious new bag. One time, I looked at the bag and I loudly said to my mother, "Mom, the bag is bleeding." My folks got very nervous and we had to exit the bus. We walked home the rest of the way, so that no one would discover the "Secret Package."

The "Secret Package" was no more than a piece of meat for our dinner, some food or other essential item that my mother had exchanged for a handmade dress.

This is how exaggerated the communist system had become. It forced us to take measures that were deemed illegal due to the lack of resources in Cuba.

During this era, you could not just go to the store and buy any food or clothing, even if you had money. A family was given a coupon book that dictated what you could buy per month and in what quantity: One pound of beef, one pound of sugar, ½ pound of coffee and so on.

The problem was not just the limitations in the book, but that often when our turn came to purchase our items, the store shelves were already empty.

This situation forced my family to deal in the black market. My parents were fully aware that getting caught in such dealings were grounds for incarceration or even worse, denying our exit from Cuba.

Obtaining proper food and clothing through the black market was dangerous but necessary. Mom would take orders for dresses, skirts or other handmade clothing and exchange them for groceries from farmers or other people who had the groceries we needed. My parents were caught a couple of times carrying groceries into the apartment. However, we were lucky that our neighborhood snitch was easily bribed. On those occasions, my mom ended up losing the bounty and making a free dress for the snitch. Getting caught and loosing the groceries we had obtained was a set back, but at least our Cuban departure papers remained in order.

In this country, kids who accompany their parents to the store often leave with some kind of toy or goody in hand. Cuban parents did not have that luxury. Going to the store with a child was torture for the child as well as the parent.

I remember one time, on a day that we were allowed to shop, my dad took my brother and me to the store. My family had been collecting empty jars of yogurt all month. Once in a while, the distributor would have extra yogurt and would stock the shelves of the local store. Since the item was close to the expiration date, yogurt was not in the ration book and could be bought by anyone at a certain quantity per person. The shopper had to bring in an empty jar for each yogurt they wanted to buy.

As my dad and I collected our yogurt, my little brother wandered away from us. My dad had never been a good babysitter. My mom would only let my mischievous brother out of her sight if she had no other recourse. We frantically searched for the little one until we spotted him in the baby aisle of the store.
My brother had grabbed a jar of baby food from the shelf. Because only infants were allowed to have baby food, my dad could not purchase the item for my brother. This news caused the 2-year-old to throw a violent tantrum. As my father tried to negotiate with my brother, the little one held on to the jar with both hands like a football receiver going for a touchdown. I remember customers at

the store laughing, but the store workers did not think it was funny. I attempted to calm my brother but I was unsuccessful as he only kicked me and screamed more loudly.

The incident started to cause such a scene that the store attendant, fearful of escalation, told my father to just take the baby food and let my brother eat it in the corner of the store. We were not allowed to leave the store with the jar of baby food so we candidly stood in the corner while my brother ate the food. A large pile of burlap sacks filled with rice provided cover for the delinquent toddler. My brother ate the baby food quickly and after he finished, I could see the expression of triumph on his face.

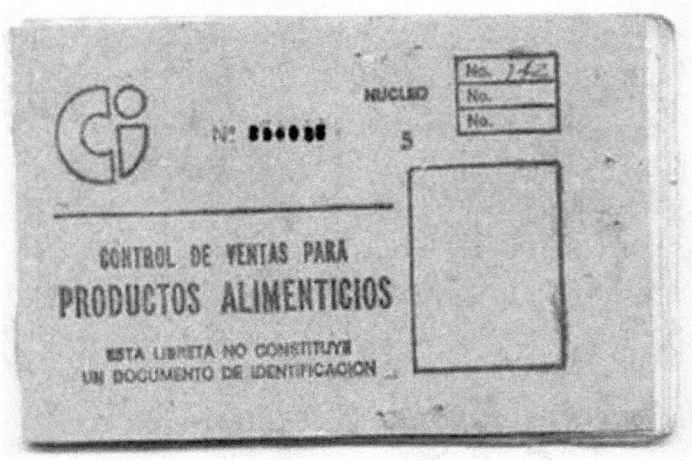

Ration coupon book

Merry Christmas

Christmas was prohibited in Cuba. Castro, however, did permit one day of sharing gifts. On January 6 of each year, Cuba celebrated "Kid's Day", although Christians still called it, "Three Wise Men Day". The Catholic catechism observes January 6 as the day three wise men came upon the manger of Baby Jesus.

Russia would usually send a ship to Cuba with toys for "Kids Day".
There were not many to go around, so Cuban children would be allowed to receive three gifts each.
The three gifts consisted of one "basic" toy, the best toy, (radio, roller skates, dolls, etc.), one "non-basic" toy (play jewelry, ball, plastic sword, etc.) and one "directed" toy (coloring book, pencils for school, etc.).
The neighborhood store would hand out numbered tickets. When our number was called, we got to choose our three toys from the available stock on the store shelves.

Most kids would already know what they would be receiving on Kid's Day. My parents, having been Americanized, made me wait until January 6 to open my gifts. I would search the entire apartment until I discovered the hideout, although I never would tell of my discovery.

My parents warned me that if I were to discover my gifts before January 6, I would receive a bag full of coal.
One year, Castro and the U.S.S.R. had a falling out. Thus, the toy ship did not come to Cuba that year.

TV stations, all three of them, would talk constantly of the importance of creativity. Castro encouraged all parents to design and make costumes for their children in lieu of buying "meaningless" toys the year that the ship did not come. He wanted the costumes to reflect the direction of the country moving towards equality and triumph. Everyone made costumes for their children; what choice did they have?

This year, on Kid's Day, the costumed children went out to play at my apartment building's garage. Every kid in my building, except me, had on a costume relating to communism. There were soldier uniforms with wooden machine guns, Che Guevara costumes, (also with guns), Castro beards and fake cigars.
I had a Robin Hood costume, sewn by my mother. I was embarrassed. I wanted to dress like the other children but my mother would not permit this. With bow and arrow in hand and a chicken feather in my cap, I was the laughing stock of the twelfth floor.

Kids would run around and shoot at me with their fake guns, making elaborate bullet sounds with their voices. I became angry and thought, "I will show them."
I put an arrow on the bow, pulled back the string, aimed, released and shot the biggest bully right in the chest. The hickory-twig arrow broke in two pieces upon striking the boy. The other kids stared in disbelief and the boy started to scream in pain. I ran back into my apartment and hid in my bed.

Moments later, the wounded bully's mother knocked on our apartment door. It was none other than the defense committee agent (the building snitch).
My dad took the bow and smashed it on the floor. No more Robin Hood for me. I was very happy.

Cuban kids go without nice toys, modern clothing and proper nutrition every year.
Food was scarce. Many nights I went to bed with just a glass of water sweetened with a couple of spoonfuls of sugar for dinner.

These circumstances are common in many parts of the world where free enterprise and meaningful employment are scarce.

The Crime

My mom made clothes in order to trade them for food, especially for my younger brother who suffered from allergies to milk and other rationed foods. My mother took matters into her own hands for our survival while my father repaired streets in the work camp under the merciless Caribbean sun.

Mom would anxiously wait for shopping day when she was allowed to purchase a few yards of fabric per month. Needing more fabric than she was allowed to buy, she developed a dangerous plan.

Mom believed that if she could fool the store by altering the purchase coupon, she could buy more fabric. After buying her share of fabric, my mom carefully went over the annotation that indicated the purchase she had made that month with an eraser until almost all of the markings had disappeared.

The next day, knowing there would be a different clerk in the store, we left our house to purchase more material.

As she handed the clerk the purchase coupon, my mother began to think about what could happen if it was discovered that she had altered the previous entry. She could be fined, sent to jail, or worse, lose our family's exit permit from Cuba.

Her nerves began to take hold of her. As she extended her arm to give the clerk the purchase book, her heart pounded faster and louder, blood rushing to her face. At the site of my nervous mother, the clerk noticed the fraud and confiscated her purchase book.

The clerk escorted my mother, my brother and me to the store's office. We walked through an endless hallway towards the rear of the building. The floor was dirty and pieces of floor tile were missing. The walls had many sheets of pinned pieces of paper, including old memos. Some, had handwriting on them, as if used to annotate a phone number or a reminder.

When we finally reached the office, we were asked to sit down and wait for the manager.

I sat on a wooden chair, but my feet did not reach the floor. My mom paced back and forth in the little room carrying my brother in her arms. The office smelled of mildew and my asthma began to flare up, causing me to use my American-bought inhaler.

There were several sheets of paper and a dirty coffee cup on the desk. On one of the walls, there was a calendar with Fidel Castro's picture on it. It had a caption that read, *"Patria o muerte Venceremos"* ("Country or death, we will persevere").

On another wall, there was a centerfold of a woman holding her dress down to keep it from flying up in the air. My mother told me it was

Marilyn Monroe. I now realize the hypocrisy of the person who poorly decorated this office.

After what seemed an eternity, a man opened the door and entered the office. Closing the door behind him, he sat down at his desk and pretended to organize some of the papers on his desk. Lighting a cigar, he put his hands behind his head and began to rock his office chair.
The man looked at my brother and me and then at my mother. He told my mother that he understood the tough situation that the country was in. He stated that he felt bad for my mother, having to resort to this petty crime in order to make ends meet. He showed my mother a written confession and told her that if she signed it, the revolution would be lenient.
It was so believable that I wanted my mom to sign it and be done with it.

My mom demanded, "What am I doing here?" The man replied, "Take it easy, I just want to get to the bottom of this, for your own good. What do you have to say about your ration book's alteration? Do you know that what you did is a crime?"
My mom told the man that she had not done anything wrong. The man told us to stay put and he left the office.

After about fifteen minutes, a woman came in. Dressed in a military uniform with a folder in her hand, the woman slammed the folder on the desk and told my mother that because of her actions, she had the power to rip my mother's American visa. My mother, with her Latin temperament, told the woman, "You are nobody to rip any government documents that have been signed by our grand leader, First Minister of Cuba, Fidel Castro".

The startled woman took out a booklet from her large purse, wrote a summons and then instructed my mother to report to the local police station for questioning, in less than a week. She then told us to leave.

The trip from the store to our apartment building was approximately four city blocks. That walk seemed endless that day. The entire trip was quiet and we did not dare say a word. I imagine my mother was thinking of every possible scenario that could play out, each of them bad; our family was in trouble.
After finally arriving home, my mom acquired a migraine so painful that she went to bed.

Between friends and family members, the news of my mom's trouble traveled to the camp where my father was working. By the time the news of my mother reached my dad, the story had changed to include that my mom was in jail for contraband, which was a total exaggeration.

My dad arrived at our home the next day and my parents stood facing each other in the hallway in total silence. The tension was so immense that I blurted out, "Mom's in trouble with the cops!" The woman who had been crying the day before stood in front of my dad, looking furiously into his eyes, and with the greatest conviction I had ever seen, lied and said, "This is a false accusation! I didn't do anything wrong!"

Thanks to my mom's cunning demeanor, my father marched straight down to the police station and demanded that the accusation be withdrawn. A person who had been a friend to my dad was working at the station as an investigator. As a favor to my dad, he managed to have all charges against my mother dropped. We dodged another bullet.

Political correctness in Cuba had reached fanaticism. There was only one acceptable point of view. If a citizen considered anything contrary to this status quo, they were labeled traitor, racist, arrogant, or worse. It seemed as if everything was a crime. If a citizen tried to sell anything of value, without going through the ration book, they could be arrested. If you installed a radio antenna, capable of reaching American stations, you could be arrested. If you voiced an opinion against the government, you could be arrested. The crime was classified as endangerment, or anti-revolutionist. The police did not respect civil rights. If a citizen was accused of being an anti-revolutionist, that citizen would be arrested, beaten and thrown in jail without a hearing. If there was a hearing, it was outrageously one-sided, as in the case of the farmer who killed a chicken.

Under this new form of government, farmlands were confiscated and the farmers were given a small salary to keep working them. One farmer killed one of his chickens to feed his family. He was arrested. At his trial, the prosecution alleged that the chicken would have been able to raise multiple chicks. Therefore, the farmer was charged with grand theft against the people and was taken to jail.

Jails in Cuba are not what citizens in the U.S. are used to seeing. In the U.S., prisoners seem to be treated fairly and actually have some rights, including balanced nutrition and security. Cuban prisons are the most deplorable places in the world. With no civil rights, prisoners undergo inhumane treatment and an abundance of physical and mental abuse.

Out of my 12th story window, I could see one of those prisons, "The Cabaña", or the Cabin. The Cabaña was a fort built by the Spaniards in the 18th century to protect the bay from pirate ships. In

Castro's Cuba, the fort is still used as a prison
where men are placed in dungeons to rot.
Sometimes, I could see the lights from the Cabaña
reflected across the waters of the Havana Bay. My
father told me that the lights only came on when a
man was being executed on the wall.
The wall he was referring to was a wall used to
execute people via a firing squad.
Cuban citizens were executed often as they were
seen as a danger to the revolution because of their
firm anti-communist convictions and beliefs.
When it came to his security, Castro had no mercy.
He executed the son of a man who had previously
pardoned Castro from prison just before he took
over Cuba.

La Cabaña (The Cabin) prison Photo by Cubanet.org

Last rights for a firing squad victim.
Photo by Cubanet.org

The Great Lie

The world outside of Cuba cannot understand what the Castro regime signifies. Living conditions in Cuba would seem horrific to anyone who has not lived through them.

The communist propaganda and the censure of all means of communication helped to keep the most horrible secret of the Caribbean; a place in the world that hides atrocities against all fundamental human rights; a portion of the earth where the light of human happiness does not reach.

Personally, I have grown tired of people asking me about the so-called free education and free healthcare of Cuba. Today in the United States, the socialist movement fills our young with the illusion of free education and healthcare. There are times when politicians use Cuba as an example of these "perks".

The truth is that the Cuban people do not have access to any medical advancement. Many cannot find relief for their ailments.

The students who take part in the communist system are allowed to enroll in the universities. These students soon find out after becoming a doctor or an engineer that they are tools of the regime. Castro rents doctors and other professionals out to other countries. The payment for the services rendered by these individuals is paid directly to Castro. The doctor only gets a small salary.

In Cuba, every citizen has the same pay in the name of equality. Currently the salary is about $60 per month.

The hospitals in Cuba that cater to foreigners and tourists charge for their care around the same rate as the U.S. does. However, Cuban citizens cannot use these hospitals. The "free" hospitals available for the Cuban people lack the most basic resources. The electricity in the hospitals is rationed and there is not enough medication available.

Anyone who is to be admitted for a procedure in a hospital is told to get the medication prior to admittance and supply their own bed linens.

I state the case of my own grandfather in Cuba. In the year 1998, I sent my grandfather medication from the U.S. Cuban doctors prescribed the medication in order for my grandfather to have a medical procedure.

Upon receiving the medication, my grandfather sold the medication in order to buy food. When my grandfather went to the hospital for his stomach ulcer treatment without the medication, the doctors could not perform the procedure.

While my grandfather waited for another shipment of the medication, he bled to death on his hospital bed.

Why sacrifice years of higher education if you cannot enjoy the fruits of your labor? Many professionals fled Cuba to other countries in search of careers in their field, only to find out they have to enroll in school again or pass a bar exam in order to get a job, something not easy to do when you have not mastered the language. Still, many have accomplished this and have left everything behind to start a new life where a man can control his own destiny.

Life becomes hopeless in the myth of equality. There's no motivation for growth, effort or dignity.

School

Cuban exiles who reside in the U.S. can observe and identify how the curriculum and social development in our schools is rapidly curving towards the left, even in the most rural areas of America.

As I see the transformation in our schools today, I remember my experiences in my Cuban school.

For a child who was leaving the country, it was difficult to cope in school. Because I was different, my classmates bullied me.
The teachers were appointed according to their loyalty to Castro and therefore would not defend me. I was a good student. I had the ability to learn and get high grades. This ability helped me to advance in school despite the stressful environment.
During recess, I would get in many fights. School kids everywhere, tend to choose uniqueness in someone in order to target them for bullying.
They called me a "worm". "Worm" was a term used for the people leaving the country. You were considered a worm because worms slither. Supposedly, I was slithering to America with no legs to stand on on my own.

One weekend, my uncle took me to the beach. I am asthmatic, so the beach was helpful to my lungs. Being a red head with fair skin, the sun's exposure gave me first-degree burns on my back that weekend.

The next day at school, I was complaining of the pain from the blisters on my back. One of the bullies overheard me and jumped me from behind. He scratched my back, further damaging my skin, and I was sent to the infirmary for my burn.

Life was not easy for a "worm" in a Cuban school. Even the teachers joined in on the torture.

I specifically remember one day when the teacher was going to give the class a lesson on religion. I remember thinking that this was odd, since any reference to God is prohibited in Cuban schools. Like in America today, God has been removed from the classroom. In Cuba, deviation from God started with the separation of church and state. After a few years of tearing down religious values in children, God eventually became prohibited. My teacher told the class to put our heads down on the desk and pray to God for candy. When we lifted our heads, there was nothing on our desks. After a long speech about the non-existence of God, the teacher once again told us to put our heads down and this time, ask the revolution for candy. When my head went up there were two pieces of candy on my desk.

I noticed that the rest of the class had plenty of

candy while I only had two pieces. My teacher, a woman whom my parents trusted with my intellectual development, explained to the class that even though I was abandoning my country, the revolution was kind to me because I was a mere victim of my parents' erroneous ideologies.

On that day, I was eight years old. I have never forgotten that moment. Those humiliating words said in front of my peers at my young and fragile age would haunt me forever. The incident did not stop there. The confusion and pain continued when I got home to tell the story. My mother now had the task of debriefing me reminding me to maintain my faith in God and my hate for the communist system. I will never forget her words to me,
 "I prefer you dead than have you become a communist".

My mom was militant. Having lived in the U.S., my mother knew of the better life beyond the waters of Cuba. She was not about to let the communist regime turn me into one of them with their psychological warfare. My mom was a radical whenever she had an opportunity to give me a lesson in communism.

Food was scarce in my home. Many times I did not like the food that was available for supper. I especially had a profound hate for grits. Without any butter or condiments, the taste of grits was disgusting to me and I refused to eat them. My mother would sit beside me with the spoon in one hand and a rubber sandal in the other. As my mom shoved the spoon full of grits into my mouth, she would repeat over and over:

"Eat this, so you never forget communism."

The Spiritual Battle

Communism prohibits every type of liberty,
including the right to practice religion.
Not only does the communist education system
abolish your faith while in school, but it also made
it difficult to practice it away from school.

People of faith are ridiculed. Parishioners are
submitted to acts of repudiation when assisting
church.
The Cuban form of the Boy Scouts, called
Pioneros or Pioneers, is used as a tool of violence
against churchgoers. Unlike the Boy Scouts, who
are taught citizenship and respect, the Pioneers are
taught to throw stones at parishioners as they enter
the temple and to insult anyone not in accordance
with the communist fanaticism.

On Sundays, my mother would dress us up and we
would head out to church. If my dad was home, he
would come too.
Knowing very well that religion is anti-
revolutionary, I knew that trouble was just around
the corner.
The trip on the bus was nice. It was not often that
I left the apartment building where we lived.
With my dad away and my mother sewing her
fingers off, there was little time for outings.

Once out of the bus, we walked a few blocks to the church. As we approached the cathedral, I would admire the impressive 18th century Spanish architecture.

The church stands on the main square of the plaza in Old Havana. It's size took up an entire city block. She was an obvious contrast to the run-down buildings around her. Once Cuba's infrastructure collapsed, there was no money to make repairs or maintenance on buildings around the city. Through either respect or fear of the Vatican, Castro stayed out of the church.

As we walked through the majestic wooden doors, the spirit of God took over.

The marble floors and golden shrines let me forget the rest of Cuba for a moment. The granite statues of the apostles and the carvings on the walls stating the Lord's Prayer gave out a supernatural aura. As the enormous pipe organ played a soft trans-like chant, I felt safe. At that moment I was standing on holy ground.

The Cathedral in Old Havana

On a particular day at church I remember there was a special service for the feast of Our lady of Charity. After mass was over, we filed out of the cathedral.

Once outside, we encountered a group of young people gathered across the sidewalk. They were shouting obscenities at the parishioners exiting the church.

It was a scary mob. They were the "Pioneers" and their scoutmasters. I had seen this similar behavior before. Although this was not unfamiliar to us, we continually allowed our faith to come first.

It was our duty to attend church on Sunday. My mom would say, "Jesus endured worse for us, it's the least we can do for Him."

We rapidly crossed the street away from the church. My mom tried to shield me and my brother from harm. The Pioneers were throwing eggs at us. One egg hit my mom on her side. She fainted and fell to the ground. One of the parishioners came to my mother's aid. Once my mother composed herself, the pioneers were gone. We walked to the bus stop and took a bus home.

That was Cuba in the 60s. Once, a 90% Christian nation, Cuba had become appalled at the notion of God.

In Castro's Cuba, pastors and priests are censored and regulated. Sometimes, if the clergy is a strong community leader, the government replaces him with a more liberal individual. The liberal clergy were accustomed to informing the authorities of all church activities. This persecution caused a decline in Christian worship. Citizens are turning to alternative practices such as voodoo or simply secularism.

Once communism removed God from Cuba's society, the morals and integrity of the people were corrupted.

Confusion

A child who expresses the desire to leave Cuba is
subjected to ridicule and abuse. Other kids did not
miss an opportunity to humiliate me as a coward
who was abandoning his country.
My father was called a traitor, a word that
resonated in my mind like a giant bell hitting
against my head.

I endured this treatment for many years, years of
anguish and bullying that a child should not have
to be subject to.

My friends were few. My parents sheltered me
against bad influences in our neighborhood.
We lived in a twelve-story building surrounded by
gossip and unjustly people.

Not all of the kids were mean to me. I was friends
with a boy of color whom my parents trusted
named Morgan. Morgan was older than me.
Several times a week, Morgan and I would go
down to the parking lot of our building to ride my
bike. Not many kids had a bicycle in our
neighborhood.
My parents brought this bicycle from the U.S.
when they returned to Cuba in 1960.
We would ride through the parking lot of the
building. Since there were very few cars stationed
there, it was a perfect place for riding. Sometimes,

other kids would come down and join us.
Morgan, being older and stronger than the other
kids, made sure I was safe from any trouble.

One day, as we sat resting on the pavement,
Morgan asked me if I would hate him when I left
for the U.S. He said that people of color were
slaves in America and were not allowed to play
with white kids.

This idea was so horrible that it startled me and I
dared not tell my parents. How could I hate my
best friend? How would I deal with this once I got
to this new place?

This was one of Castro's many tactics. The media
in Cuba was censured and still is. TV and radio
were full of communist propaganda. Castro
controlled the masses through the media. As in the
U.S., the media is credited for driving the people.
Cuban television programs would portray white
policemen in the U.S. as beating Black civilians on
the streets, with sticks. Television would play
movies showing people of color having to use
different bathrooms and water fountains in
American clubs. We saw movies showing blacks
as slaves in houses owned by white families.
Castro accused the U.S. of mistreatment of blacks
through public hangings.
While there were terrible things going on in the
60s to Black or African American people, it was

not slavery and there were no public hangings.

Once I left Cuba, I never saw Morgan again. I would love to reunite with him and tell him about today's great strides in the U.S. civil rights movement.

Family

Some weekends we would go and visit my grandmother and my cousins who lived in another town. The bus ride and some walking was part of the fun. Throughout the week I would keep my sanity by thinking of the upcoming weekend. At last, I would get a break from the torture and enjoy family fun.

My cousins lived on a hilltop. We played, ran and laughed. We engineered a cardboard magic carpet to slide down the hill at full speed. For brakes, we crashed into the flat ground at the bottom of the hill. We did not have baseballs nor bats, so we played stickball with any piece of wood we could find. We used flattened cans for bases.
On one occasion, I found a roller skate. It was the type of skate you would put on the bottom of your shoe and secure it with a skate key.
I could not wait to show it to my cousins. Once at my cousins' house, we took the skate apart and nailed it to a board. I do not remember whose idea it was to roll down the hill on the skateboard, but I ended up being the test pilot.
As I was going down the hill, the skate board began to pick up speed. This was not like the cardboard carpet. The skate came off the board and I ended the trip on my belly. My hands and knees were sore for days, but the thrill was priceless.

These were the best times of my life. But as in every occasion of my life in Cuba, the joy was ephemeral.

My aunt, the mother of my cousins, was a communist sympathizer. She taught her children a different ideology than my mother taught me. At the end of the weekend, my cousins would complain and ask me why I wanted to abandon them. They would try to coerce me into staying in Cuba. My heart was torn between wanting to be with my extended family and my desire to leave.

The trip back to our apartment was no longer a happy trip. Once back in our concrete and steel cage, I would cry at the thought of leaving my cousins. Even today, over 40 years later, I still have not seen my cousins.

That is another reality of Castro's system, the separation of families. Not only are you abused because you desire to leave but Castro makes sure you suffer for your decision for the rest of your life.

Imagine mourning the death of your grandfather from another country because you are not permitted to return to your own homeland to properly bury your dead.

In recent developments, the U.S. has normalized

some relations with Cuba. Now, Americans can travel to Cuba. For a naturalized Cuban that is not the same option. Even though I am a naturalized American citizen, I am considered a Cuban while in Cuba. This is Castro's rule. I would have no protection from the U.S. while traveling in Cuba. After everything we went through in Cuba in order to come to the U.S., I would never give a penny to a communist government.

When a Cuban citizen applies to come to the U.S., the U.S. Government performs a background check. The exiled must establish a bank account and secure employment prior to being accepted. Once the American residency is approved in the U.S., Castro can authorize the whole family to leave, or just part of it. Many people have left loved ones behind in an effort to save some family members from communism. Some citizens even send their children alone in an effort to give them a better future.

From December 1960 to October 1962, fourteen thousand unaccompanied children came to the United States without their parents in a humanitarian operation called *"Pedro Pan"*. Half of the children were reunited with family members in the U.S. and the other half were placed in homes through an organization called "Catholic Charities".

These were desperate measures that mothers would

take in order to save their children from communism.

Happy Birthday

A birthday celebration in the U.S. is so commonplace that a party is generally expected. Usually, a party may include clowns, gifts, food and even a DJ. There is plenty of food and party favors to go around for everyone. This was not the case for me in Cuba.

How can we instill the value of a birthday party in an American child? For a person of any age, it is unfathomable to think there could come a day when a birthday party becomes a luxury.

In Cuba, for your birthday, you were allowed to buy a cake and some pastries. However, it was not an easy task. A person would have to wait for a cake, sometimes an entire night, to be able to purchase one.

I remember my 6th birthday party. My dad traveled 27 kilometers (16.7 miles) to a bakery to take a number and wait in line all night outside the store to buy a cake the next morning. Due to the shortage of ingredients to bake the cakes, the baker could not bake enough cakes for everyone in line. While my dad spent the night at the bakery, my mom fixed up the house for the party. When the guests arrived, my mother tried to entertain us with games and songs. I remember running around the house with friends, yelling in chorus, "We want cake, we want cake!"

Hours went by without cake and my mother did
not know what to do to keep the restless kids from
mutiny.
We did not have many toys and the ones we did
have were already boring to us. Mom concocted
some candy out of sugar and water on the stove.
We watched and waited until the cooled treat was
ready to eat. It was wonderful. I was the star of
the party because my mom was a genius.

I learned later that when my father finally got his
turn back at the bakery, the store had run out of
cakes. Knowing he could show up without a cake,
my dad began to negotiate with other customers
already served. After offering a large amount of
money, probably his week's salary, he convinced a
customer to sell him their cake.
The baker quickly took the cake, removed the
name of the child who would have no cake that
day, and replaced it with my name.

When the cake finally arrived at the party, we all
yelled and applauded. My dad, who had been
awake for twenty-four hours, took a bath, got
dressed, came out to blow out the candles with us
and plummeted onto the sofa where he slept for the
rest of the event.

While I had fun at my birthday parties, my parents

became increasingly worried. If I were to reach the age of fifteen before leaving Cuba, I would have to stay behind.

In Cuba, once a male child reaches fifteen years of age, he is drafted into the military. Many children were sent to fight overseas in other communist countries like Angola and Venezuela. This draft was another reason why my parents grew more anxious with each passing year.

My parents used to put one less candle on the birthday cake to confuse the neighbors into thinking I was one year younger, assuming it would buy me one more year. A futile attempt I am sure, since the government probably had my correct age in their records.

At ten years old, life in Cuba was becoming a bit easier to manage. Thanks to my older age and my parents' influence, I learned to avoid some of the controversial situations.

I learned to shift political conversations to more benign matters. I used jokes to defuse arguments. By necessity, I became a master of diversions. My mother called me the "politician" of the family.

Towards the end of my time in Cuba, life was more tolerable for me. When things became challenging, I would lose myself in my thoughts to the day that I would finally be leaving the country.

Everything seemed temporary; soon I would go to the Promised Land.

The Departure

They say God knows best. That phrase was never so true until the time of our departure from Cuba. I think that God's plan for me was to insure my convictions and conservative ideologies by putting before me the most stringent of tests. The last part of my journey in Cuba put the nail on the coffin for me.

Today, I thank the good Lord for delivering me through such a rocky desert in order to define me forever.

Upon the soldiers' arrival at our Havana apartment, the news of our departure approval was bittersweet. I experienced feelings of joy as well as fear.

From our apartment's balcony, I could see the agents coming from the bus stop. Two men, in olive green uniforms, exited the bus. One man was taller than the other. The shorter guy was carrying a brief case. They were dressed differently than our neighbors and were easy to spot. The long-sleeved shirts in the middle of June gave them away. They wore cargo-style pants, tucked in black military boots.

The distance from the bus stop to the apartment building was approximately a quarter of a mile.

I rushed out and took my bicycle to Morgan's apartment. I wanted him to keep it when I left Cuba. Once you were told to leave, you could not give away anything you owned. The agent of the neighborhood committee, or neighborhood snitch, brought a list of all the personal belongings we had acquired through our life in Cuba. If anything was missing from this list, we would forfeit our departure. I remember my mom having a broken teapot in a drawer. The pieces of ceramic were proof that we had not sold it or given it away. Once a citizen left Cuba, the government would distribute the citizen's personal belongings to other communist citizens in need.

The men in green military uniforms gave me the shakes. My mother rushed to get our clothes from the closet as the cops inventoried everything in the apartment.
The neighborhood rat quickly demanded to see the bike and Morgan had to surrender it to the authorities.

Once the inventory was over, the soldiers put a seal on the apartment door and we left to my aunt's house, where I said my last goodbye to my dear cousins.
My father got word at the work camp and reunited with us a day later.

We arrived at the airport in Varadero for final

processing. There, they stripped us and searched our bodies and luggage. It was a horrible sight watching the woman, in the military uniform, tear up our prized family photographs. There was no point in destroying the photographs other than to inflict mental abuse in the hope that we would retaliate and cause a scene preventing us from departure. At one point, the woman took out a small statue of the Virgin Mary from my mother's bag and threw it on the floor, destroying it into a million pieces.

Inside the statue was a small gold chain that my mother hid in case we needed to sell it for money later. The woman confiscated it. The only money we had was a Cuban nickel that I managed to keep in my pants' pocket, a coin that I still cherish as my only childhood relic from Cuba.

Cuban Nickel, five cent coin

All Aboard

After a long and stressful day, the time came to board the plane. Just a few feet from the door that led to the runway, a Swiss doctor gave us our physical check-up. He looked at my four-year-old brother and told my mother that he could not board the plane.

My brother had just gotten over the chicken pox and had one little blister left between two fingers on his right hand. The soldier beside the doctor looked at my brother's hand and told us he could not leave Cuba. I remember the look on the doctor's face as if he were apologizing for sealing my brother's fate.

So much sacrifice, so much tribulation, so much agony, so many prayers and now, this. At the end of the journey, one tiny blister would render all in vain. I could only imagine that my mother's faith was shattering, although my mother never expressed any vacillation in her beliefs.

My mother, with the firmness of a Roman soldier, composed herself and told my dad, *"Take Pete and go. We can save at least one"*.

My dad stood there in disbelief. My mother's eyes seemed to go through his own like a sword of fire. I will never forget that moment. The agent told my father to leave and take me. He said my mother would be given a room at the airport hotel until my brother was well enough to travel and then she would follow us.

I did not believe there was much credibility in what that agent said, but my dad knew what he had to do. He kissed my mother and my brother. My mom hugged and kissed me, told me to be strong, and then we headed for the airplane leaving my mother and my brother behind.

As I boarded up the stairs of the Eastern Airlines DC3, a shiny silver twin-engine propeller aircraft, I did not look back.
Once I took my seat, I decided to look for my mother. I could barely see through the window. I saw the terminal through the window, but my mother was not there. My father remained silent and his gaze was fixed outside of that little window, like he was in a trance. I did not dare speak. When all passengers were seated, two armed Cuban guards walked through the cabin looking at each passenger. It was tense. I just stared at the seat in front of me and did not move. My parents had advised me that if the soldiers saw me crying, I would not get to leave. Castro had declared any child that appeared to be saddened by having to leave would be considered under duress and would stay in Cuba.

So many things passed through my mind at that moment partnered with feelings of joy and sadness.

I thought of my cousins who had begged me not to abandon them. But at last, I would be free.

I was going to a land where people claimed the Coca Colas would magically get cold upon being opened and dollar bills were found on the ground.

The soldiers left the plane and the doors closed. The pilot accelerated down the runway and the engines roared. The flight attendant looked like an angel with blond hair and pale skin. Her eyes were blue like the marbles I played with as a younger child. She looked at me and smiled as she passed by my seat. I thought, "Maybe this is heaven!"

As the aircraft taxied down the runway, I thought, "This is it. Soon I will be making new friends." I looked out the window and said, *"Goodbye my beautiful Cuba."* I do not know why I said that, perhaps I had heard it in a song.

The steel bird lifted off the ground with a deafening sound. Gravity pulled me deep into the seat. What a euphoric feeling.

As soon as the plane leveled off, the captain came on the radio and said, in a funny sounding Spanish, *"Bienvenidos a America"* (Welcome to America).

The silence was broken. The passengers began to

scream and clap. It was like a stadium roar.
"Viva America!, Viva Jesus Christ!, To hell with Communism!" The passengers were hugging and kissing. Singing and laughing. It was so contagious that I started to clap too. My head was like an oscillating radar, tracking the entire cabin, until my eyes came upon my father's face. He was neither yelling nor clapping. He was frozen looking through that window, pale as a ghost.

At that moment, reality hit me. My feelings of joy and enthusiasm quickly turned to anguish. I had just realized the horror in my father's eyes. I would never see my mother and brother again.

The rest of the trip was tense. I did not speak. After a couple of hours, we arrived in Miami, Florida.
A shuttle took us to a building in downtown Miami called "Liberty Tower". There, my father interviewed with American agents. These agents did not wear uniforms, but dressed in nice suits and spoke English. I assume my father did not want me to hear about my mother. Even though I thought I could speak English, having learned words like *television, telephone and sonofabitch*, I understood nothing.

We were given a box with a toothbrush, toothpaste, a pastry and a "cafe con leche", which is a common Cuban drink consisting of whole milk with a shot of espresso coffee in it. It was the best beverage I had ever had.

Once all paperwork was over, we were handed over to our waiting family members. I met new cousins whom I had never known.
I watched as my dad embraced his sisters and family for the first time in nine years. They had been in the U.S. since the early 60's, when Castro took over Cuba. There were plenty of hugs, kisses and tears. Everyone was jubilant at the encounter. Like most Cuban families, we all tried to talk at the same time, and we continually grew louder. If the American agents had not been used to these scenes, they would have thought we were fighting.

My mother did not have any family in the U.S. at the time of my arrival. I was afraid her absence would not matter to these people I had just met. Thinking about her kept me from fully enjoying the festive moment.
The family had come in various cars. My dad and I got into my cousin's 1969 Buick Riviera. It was a strange looking car. The car had a v-shaped trunk. It looked like a space vehicle compared to the old vintage cars from the 50's that I was used to seeing in Cuba.

Eastern Airlines DC3

Freedom Tower Miami, FL

Welcome to America

On the way to my aunt's house, our new home, we stopped at a grocery store. Upon entering the store, I felt a strong wind of air conditioning fill my frail, asthmatic lungs. It was like breathing for the first time in my life.

In front of me was a fruit stand full of oranges and apples. It was as tall as the sky. They let me push the grocery cart. My uncle only needed a few items that he had forgotten to buy, but I insisted on going down every isle. My mind could not fathom this place. There was not only bread, but an entire aisle of bread. I saw cans containing all sorts of foods, some of which I had no idea what they were. There was milk and juice and oh yes, yogurt.
Excited, I told my dad, "Dad there's a whole section for dog food!" He looked at me and wept sadly. Dogs in the U.S. eat better than we did in Cuba.

How could anyone decide what to buy?
My cousin told me, "You can get whatever you want and as many of them as you like."
I will never forget that moment.

The next day I heard the adults talking about my mother's fate. My Cuban aunt, the communist one, had a telephone and my mother used it to call us.

To make a phone call from Cuba, my mother would request a phone line from the Cuban operator. After a few hours of wait, the operator would facilitate a connection from Cuba to the U. S. It seems that as soon as we left, she and my brother were thrown out into the streets like dogs. The empty promise of the agent did not last an hour. As my mom walked through the dark of the night, with my brother in her arms, a bus driver stopped and picked them up. My brother had developed a fever and they were six hours away from Havana. The bus driver told my mom that drivers were allowed to reserve one seat for their family members and told my mom to use the seat as if she were part of his family. My mom took the seat and with my brother on her lap, she headed home. To my Cuban family's surprise, my mother and my brother arrived at my grandmother's house hours later.
Once she knew she was safely there, she collapsed with exhaustion.

Our next few days were busy making trips to the American embassy and immigration office.
Those were days of anguish for me. How would we get my mom home? The counselor explained that there was little they could do for my mom in Cuba. Castro played by his own set of rules, much different than a civilized country. Most of my father's conversations with the counselor were in English so I could not understand, but I could still

see the disappointment in my father's eyes.
During the day, I kept busy playing with my new
cousins. They were about my age but because
their parents immigrated to the U.S. when I was 2-
years-old, I did not remember them. My cousins
had acclimated well in the U.S. Their Anglo
friends quickly took me in as part of their clan and
insisted on teaching me English. They told me
some words they had learned in Spanish. They
were words I could not repeat. We laughed at one
another's pronunciation. They taught me to play
basketball, although I was not very good. When it
was my turn to teach them how to play stickball, I
got even.

The nights were different. I shared a room with
my cousins. After much talking, my aunt would
come in the room and turn off the lights. It was
then, in the dead of silence, when I would cover
my face and cry myself to sleep.
I began to feel feelings of guilt. Had I been a good
boy to my mother? Memories of fighting with my
younger sibling haunted me. I was four years
older than my brother. Many times, I had avoided
him while playing with kids my age. He was a
handful. Back in our Havana apartment, I would
be on guard while turning every corner. I never
knew what devious trap he had in store for me.
But now, things I once did not like about my
brother I missed terribly.

One evening, I heard a conversation between my dad and my uncle. My dad was filling out an application for registration into the U.S. Military. The U.S. Selective Service, or the "Draft", was still in force in 1969. Now, I thought, I would really be alone. Why did we have to come to this country? Where was my mom?

Today, as an adult and parent, I am an advocate for children counseling during a crisis. Kids need someone to talk to and to help them understand life's curveballs. Situations in life we deem trivial can be life-changing experiences to a child. Back in '69, I had no one to talk to.

Miraculously, my mother and brother were finally able to leave the country and reunite with us in America.

I would now be able to leave behind that part of my life. The struggles would soon heal, but the experience served me to be cautious of the political climate everywhere in the world.

I quickly assimilated into this great nation, the United States of America. I made new friends and learned the language fairly quickly.
I will never forget a day at the park, when an African-American kid joined us to play. Finally, the last Communist lie had been discovered. I wish I could tell Morgan how wrong he was.

I could never hate him.

My parents continued their dream as if the eight years had been a mere interruption in our lives. Working hard day and night, my parents managed to sponsor and bring other family members from Cuba. After a few years, we owned our first home and my folks had finally opened up their own business making kitchen cabinets. Alas, the American Dream.

The Danger

In a socialist or communist system like Cuba, your own people enslave you. You are marginalized just for having different ideas. Socialists are intolerant people and most have little to lose. They will destroy our democratic way of life just to be able to play in the arena without paying for a ticket. The left will chip away at our moral and religious values in order to be accepted for the outrageous things they do, and all is in the name of "equality".

That type of life we had in Cuba is incomprehensible to American children. Those who have not lived in the jaws of socialism can never understand that the danger is very real.

If we look back at the last couple of decades in the U.S., we can see a chart of progressiveness that swings its bar slowly, but steadily, to the left.

Much of what happened in Cuba in the last fifty years is now happening in the U.S., and few are accepting this truth. Things such as intimidation tactics by community organizers, leftist watchdogs in organizations, the injection of liberal propaganda in school lesson plans, boycotts of organizations with opposing points of views, unruly protests to prevent others' rights and persecution of religious organizations are just a few similarities between Castro's government and what is happening in the U.S. today.

In the tale of the frog that was placed in a kettle of water and slowly put to the fire, the temperature of the water is slowly rising but the frog does not notice. Arrogance and indifference, coupled with government bribes through our welfare system, keeps the masses entertained and carefree.

Like the pieces in a puzzle, socialism continues to inject itself throughout the world. It's pieces are beginning to find a way to fit into America's puzzle.

The U.S. has the strongest economical system in the world, but we are not infallible.
If history is to repeat itself, as it often does, let us not forget that America suffered a great depression in 1929.
The economy entered an ordinary recession during the summer of 1929 as consumer spending dropped and unsold goods began to pile up, slowing production. Banks failed and Americans lost their money. Half of the country was unemployed. This crisis lasted for around ten years.
Not long ago, America went through another scare. This time, the government used tax dollars to bail out the banks (which in my view, misused the money) and returned to unsafe practices.

Banks continue to lend money to individuals who could not pay it back.
How many times will we bail out these institutions? Our national debt is in the trillions of dollars. Almost half of every dollar we have is owned by enemies of the U.S.

Excessive government subsidies and regulation cause tax increases. In turn, this shrinks industries' bottom line, causing consumer prices to soar or the company to move away, leaving many without employment.

A catastrophic collapse in our economy would be the end of the advancements we now enjoy. Who is going to bail us out?

Watching current events in the news, I get the feeling that many countries hate America, and it seems to stem from envy or jealousy for American resolve.

These entities would love for America to fall at the hands of a failed socialism.

Our children do not see it, but I do. It is our responsibility to stop the madness. Parents need to stop trying to be their kids' "cool friends" in fear of rejection and start being parents. As parents, we should be teaching our kids values and explaining to them why things are actually different than what is being presented to them through the media and school. If we as parents feel that social liberalism is hurting America, then we should talk to our children about the consequences that a leftist form of government can bring upon our nation. More importantly, we need to be more American. In the last decade, America has decayed to the point that our young generations are ashamed of our country. Foreign ideologies are viewed as the new goal for America. If America was that bad, millions would not still be trying to flock to her.

Our future is being shaped by the evil powers of greed and hate. Socialism is failing all around the globe and money is running out. The parasites look to America as the last pot of gold to be taken.

Pride and effort are being substituted by government handouts and apathy. The family example has been taken over by liberal social media. Our grandfathers' wisdom has been replaced with the advice of an unknown author on the World Wide Web. Religious virtues are substituted by ego and disorder.

Modern families are being devoured by the merry-go-round system of the almighty dollar. Both parents are out of the home and our children's babysitter is Hollywood's television.

I have noticed the influence of the leftists'

Hollywood agenda in most modern television programs.
Subtle messages and symbols are being put in programs so that viewers, especially children, are hearing messages they are consciously unaware of.

Sesame Street has been noted for a gross portion of these leftist political agendas that try to indoctrinate our children into the liberal mindset, Topics range from 9/11 to gun control and more.

Finding Nemo portrays humans as the beasts against the poor fish in a war between human consumption and preservation of sea life. The film does not explain how the U.S. leads in the effort on ecological awareness in the world.

Ice Age drives home the global warming alarms of the left.

Superman IV argues the harm of nuclear weapons as superman tries to take all nukes into the sun.

Although the concept of a peaceful world and environmental responsibility should be the goal of all people, these shows depict a one-sided solution without exploring some of its negative consequences.
Nuclear disarmament would work if other nations would not be trying to destroy us.
Fishing regulations would save our sea life if the

world outside the U.S. would be forced to comply with environmental laws.

China is one of the worst environmental violators in the world, yet the U.S. offers the Chinese trillions of dollars in trade benefits while turning a blind eye to these violations.

Gun violence would be curtailed if existing gun laws would be enforced. I believe that when guns are outlawed, only outlaws will have guns.

Chicago, one of the toughest gun control cities in America, is credited with one of the highest crime rates in America.

TV shows like **Quantico** portray this Utopian diversity of recruits inside the FBI training facility.

I observed, first hand, the failures of Affirmative Action. While working 23 years for the U.S. Department of Justice, I witnessed how qualified applicants were rejected and replaced with individuals with less qualifications and work ethics. When the hiring process focused on filling a diversity quota instead of qualifications, the system failed. Customer service declined and production goals were not met due to an incapable workforce.

Diversity is the key to creativity and innovation but we should not reward incompetence or dismiss achievement in the name of diversity.

I agree with teaching our children tolerance and acceptance of others. These values should be

learned in the home, under the parent's direction. I believe that parents are the best educators to open the mind of a child to exploration, while maintaining family values and costumes.
We are delegating this important formation to a plague of immorality that teaches our kids to hate their roots in order to achieve their progressive agenda.

Many TV shows try to confuse their audience as well. There is a scene in the television series, **Blue Bloods,** where a picture of Che Guevara is hanging on the wall of a Catholic school classroom. Talk about an oxymoron.
I would assume that many kids today who wear Che Guevara t-shirts do not even know that Che was the worst assassin and hit man for Fidel Castro. Guevara was a narcissist credited for a massacre of Christians via firing squads as well as by his own hand.

Leftist search engines on the Internet will downplay Che Guevara's psychotic appetite for killing. I say, go to the source and ask a Cuban exile about Che and you will find countless stories of Che's wake of executed patriots whose crimes were only to love freedom and oppose dictatorship. Below is a quote from Che Guevara's diaries:

"Crazy with fury I will stain my rifle red while slaughtering any enemy that falls in my hands! My nostrils dilate while savoring the acrid odor of gunpowder and blood. With the deaths of my enemies I prepare my being for the sacred fight and join the triumphant proletariat with a bestial howl!"

"Hatred as an element of struggle; unbending hatred for the enemy, which pushes a human being beyond his natural limitations, making him into an effective, violent, selective, and cold-blooded killing machine. This is what our soldiers must become ..." Che Guevara

Parents rarely supervise what their children are watching on television.

Kids have become more independent, therefore they are making more of their own decisions at earlier ages. When I was growing up, my parent's word was final. Today our kids demand respect without earning it.

How can we save the nation of our forefathers? We can triumph by standing up for America. We must act now.

All it takes is for us to pause, sit down and decide what role we want to take in saving our country. If we look outside our window at the rest of the world, we can see the way they are living. Is that what we want to become?

When Cuban exiles came to America, they decided to take advantage of the freedom they yearned for for so long. Never taking anything for granted, our experience with socialism is the factor of our determination.

There are no more than one million Cubans in America, making them one of, if not the smallest Hispanic group, in the U.S. Our resolve turned us into an unstoppable force. There are more Cubans in congress, the senate, local politics and fortune 500 enterprises in the U.S. than any other Hispanic group. This is not because Cubans are better or smarter than any other person, but because we know the alternative result of resting on our laurels. We face the ghosts of our history and do not want a repetition of those failures. We recognize God's desires for humanity to prosper and triumph. Cubans, unlike some other immigrated groups, know the importance of American assimilation. Most importantly, we prosper because of our appreciation and unconditional love for America. God, family and country are the driving forces we must draw from.

We should hold our representatives accountable and stand up to protest the injustices.
We should denounce all violations of our constitution and take the time to get informed, not by the liberal press, but by the grass-roots opposition. I find it difficult to see younger

generations listen to the oppositional points of view provided by the media.

University students are becoming left wing fanatics. Today, U.S. schools are condoning student disturbances that prevent opposing speech. I watched, in the news, how student protesters swarmed California State University in Los Angeles to barricade the entrances of a theater where conservative commentator, Ben Shapiro, was set to deliver a speech about censorship and diversity on college campuses. The hundreds of demonstrators, including some professors, poured into the Student Union building to block other students from attending the event.
Instead, these high-cost institutions should be encouraging dialog among the classes. How else can we open the minds of our future generation?

We need to learn from the minds of people of all ideals, both good and bad. Napoleon and Martin Luther King Jr. had the same message. *The world suffers a lot. Not because the violence of bad people. But because of the silence of the good people.*

We should start with restoring order and discipline in our homes, even when it is painful to enforce. In the story of Pinocchio, kids are being turned against their parents and encouraged to be defiant. Parents are now taught to believe that they have no control of their children's actions and decisions. Not true. If you support them, you can guide them. We must make our voices heard in our home through loving dialog, patience and good examples.

It will take time and effort to turn the wheel of America back toward the right. The train is going too fast for sharp turns. Slowing down the train means applying principles, one at a time.

If we start researching our candidates before the elections, we can support the right person for the job.

We must act at the first sign of school misguidance or social injustice. We must do it together as one undivided nation.

If we respond as a nation, we can be an unstoppable force. America has always triumphed in the face of adversity. We are used to fighting the obvious dangers we can see but the war today is much different. We are fighting a faceless enemy that lurks in the corners of our own neighborhoods. We must learn to seek out these microbes and stop them in their tracks. Only then can we start heading in the right direction.

My life finally turned around even when facing greater obstacles than Americans face now. It is possible to escape the monster. All we need to do is care about the future. If we put our priorities in order, we can persevere.

Take it from a guy that has been in the belly of the beast and survived; an exiled Cuban immigrant with a first-hand view of the puzzle.

About the Author

Pedro (Pete) Diaz was born in Cuba in 1958. In the summer of 1969, at the age of ten, he immigrated to the United States with his parents.

After graduating high school, he became an American Citizen. He married and has a daughter and a son.

Pete retired from the U.S. Department of Justice after 23 years of service and now lives in a small ranch in Texas where he owns and operates a photography business with his wife.

In his spare time, he volunteers for several local charities including civic clubs, church and veterans' affairs.

Pete continues to get involved in local politics by sharing his experiences.

INDEX